I Love Sports

Track and Field

by Kaitlyn Duling

FINISH

Bullfrog Books

Ideas for Parents and Teachers

Bullfrog Books let children practice reading informational text at the earliest reading levels. Repetition, familiar words, and photo labels support early readers.

Before Reading

- Discuss the cover photo. What does it tell them?

- Look at the picture glossary together. Read and discuss the words.

Read the Book

- "Walk" through the book and look at the photos. Let the child ask questions. Point out the photo labels.

- Read the book to the child, or have him or her read independently.

After Reading

- Prompt the child to think more. Ask: Have you ever participated in track and field? What was your favorite event?

Bullfrog Books are published by Jump!
5357 Penn Avenue South
Minneapolis, MN 55419
www.jumplibrary.com

Library of Congress Cataloging-in-Publication Data

Names: Duling, Kaitlyn, author.
Title: Track and field / by Kaitlyn Duling.
Description: Minneapolis, Minnesota: Jump!, Inc., [2018] | Series: I love sports | Includes index.
Audience: Ages: 5–8. | Audience: Grades: K to Grade 3. | Identifiers: LCCN 2017029844 (print) LCCN 2017025735 (ebook) | ISBN 9781624966729 (ebook) | ISBN 9781620318249 (hardcover: alk. paper) | Subjects: LCSH: Track and field—Juvenile literature. | Classification: LCC GV1060.55 (print) LCC GV1060.55 .D85 2018 (ebook) | DDC 796.42—dc23
LC record available at https://lccn.loc.gov/2017029844

Editor: Jenna Trnka
Book Designer: Leah Sanders
Photo Researcher: Leah Sanders

Photo Credits: FS Stock/Shutterstock, cover; hanapon1002/iStock, 1; Evikka/Shutterstock, 3; Gareth Brown/Getty, 4; SerrNovik/iStock, 5, 6–7, 16, 23br; Andy Nowack/iStock, 8, 23mr; Don Mason/Getty, 9; Denis Kuvaev/Shutterstock, 10–11, 23ml; Denys Kuvaiev/Alamy, 12–13, 23tl; JaySi/Shutterstock, 14–15; baona/iStock, 17; Sergey Novikov/Shutterstock, 18–19, 23tr; PCN Photography/Alamy, 20–21, 23bl; vectorfusionart/Shutterstock, 22tl; photofriday/Shutterstock, 22bl; Longchalerm Rungruang/Shutterstock, 22tr; Ilya Kamaukhov/Shutterstock, 22br; cherrus/Shutterstock, 24.

Printed in the United States of America at Corporate Graphics in North Mankato, Minnesota.

Table of Contents

Let's Go!

Grab your shoes. It's time for track and field.

Let's go!

Today is the
big meet.

There are
many events.

First we stretch.

Sam sprints.
He is fast!

Mae does hurdles.
She leaps high.

Joy does the long jump.

She runs.

She leaps.

She will land in the sand pit.

Joy jumps far!

sand pit

Dan does the
high jump.

He runs.

He leaps over
the bar.

He jumps high!

13

Meg runs far.

The race is long.

She runs and runs.

Some do relays. They share the race. They each run one part.

They pass a baton.

Rae's team is fast!
She crosses the
finish line.

Rae's team wins!

Do you want to try?
Run. Jump. Throw.
Track and field
is fun!

At the Track

baton

lanes

hurdles

starting blocks

Picture Glossary

high jump
An event in which athletes jump as high as they can, clearing a bar.

relays
Races in which runners each run part of a race, passing a baton.

long jump
An event in which athletes jump as far as they can.

sprints
Runs very fast for a short distance.

meet
An event at which athletes compete.

stretch
To extend the body or limbs, often to get ready for a sporting event.

Index

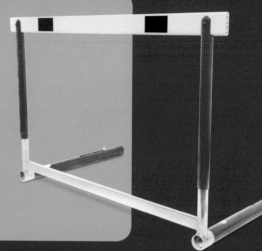

To Learn More

Learning more is as easy as 1, 2, 3.

1) Go to www.factsurfer.com

2) Enter "trackandfield" into the search box.

3) Click the "Surf" button to see a list of websites.

With factsurfer.com, finding more information is just a click away.